W9-ALK-405

Great Minds of Science

Margaret Mead

Pioneer of Social Anthropology

John Bankston

Enslow Publishers, Inc.
40 Industrial Road
Box 398
Berkeley Heights, NJ 07922
USA

http://www.enslow.com

Library of Congress Cataloging-in-Publication Data

Bankston, John, 1974-
    Margaret Mead : pioneer of social anthropology / by John Bankston.
      p. cm. — (Great minds of science)
    Includes bibliographical references and index.
    ISBN 0-7660-2507-1
    1. Mead, Margaret, 1901-1978—Juvenile literature. 2. Women
anthropologists—United States—Biography—Juvenile literature.
3. Women anthropologists—Polynesia—Biography—Juvenile literature.
I. Title. II. Series.
GN21.M36B36 2006
301'.092—dc22

                               2005020874

Printed in the United States of America

10 9 8 7 6 5 4 3 2 1

To Our Readers:
We have done our best to make sure all Internet Addresses in this book were
active and appropriate when we went to press. However, the author and the
publisher have no control over and assume no liability for the material
available on those Internet sites or on other Web sites they may link to. Any
comments or suggestions can be sent by e-mail to comments@enslow.com or
to the address on the back cover.

Illustration Credits: Courtesy of the Institute for Intercultural
Studies, pp. 7, 8, 14, 20, 22, 25, 31, 68, 79, 84, 106; Enslow Publishers,
Inc., p. 10; Everett Collection, Inc., p. 1; The Image Works, pp. 49,
112; Library of Congress, pp. 33, 40, 56, 61, 89, 101, 110; National
Archives, p. 95.

Cover Illustration: Everett Collection, Inc. (foreground); Shutter
Stock, Inc. (background).

Contents

The First Storm

THE HURRICANE STRUCK ON NEW YEAR'S Day. It arrived without warning, cutting a swath across the islands of Samoa. It swamped boats, destroyed primitive homes, and ended lives. Arriving from the Pacific Ocean, the storm crossed over the United States naval base before tearing through the jungle.

Native Samoans desperately sought shelter. In their midst, an American woman reluctantly crouched inside a water tank as the hurricane swept over. At twenty-four years old, her petite frame and casually frizzy hair made her seem much younger. Later she described the brief moment when the eye of the storm passed over and she stepped out, saying, "the air seemed chocked full of coconut leaves so stiff they might

5

have been wired. Even the sand was suspended in the embrace of that calm." The eye passed and the violence of the hurricane returned— "tearing that little calm into a thousand pieces. It was pouring rain and the air was full of flying sand, coconuts, parts of tin roofs and so on."[1]

Mead was not scared. She was angry.

Nature had interrupted her work, work that was just beginning to go well. She had no idea what would happen if her living quarters were destroyed. There was nowhere else in the village that she would be allowed to stay.

Young Rebel

Margaret Mead had arrived on the Samoan island of Ta'u that November ninth. She had begun studying the language only a few weeks before. She had never spent a night alone. Her father had paid for the trip; her school refused to fund the expedition. Her goal was to write about teenage rebellion. Although she was an adult, Mead was still rebelling.

She had rebelled against her father when he

Margaret Mead appears in native dress, between two native girls, on the island of Samoa circa 1926.

tried to talk her out of attending college. She rebelled against male anthropologists who thought the jungle too dangerous for a woman. And soon she would write a book that rebelled against the social conventions that determined the way young women and men are raised in the United States.

Before she was thirty she would be famous.

A 1928 photograph taken by Margaret Mead of some young men of Pere Village in the Manus Islands.

But arriving on Ta'u with a few cotton dresses and some notebooks, all she wanted was to prove she could handle the job. Like an ancient explorer, Mead traveled into uncharted territory, her goal to observe and try to reach reasonable conclusions.

In Search of Peace

For centuries, the diaries and other writings of explorers informed the world about the lives of native peoples. Men like Marco Polo and Christopher Columbus kept detailed records of their adventures. This was the closest most of their readers ever got to dangerous and distant lands. Unfortunately, there were few stories about peaceful natives; most focused on tribes who practiced headhunting or cannibalism.

Scottish physician Mungo Park's *Travels into the Heart of Africa*, published in 1799, detailed his explorations and love for the continent. Sadly, he was best remembered for his untimely end—the trip's sponsor went on a rescue mission hoping to

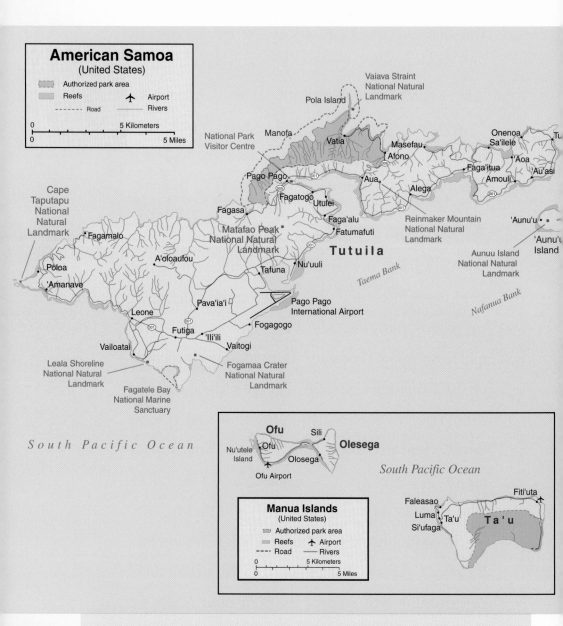

A map of Samoa and the Manua Islands. All of these islands are considered part of Polynesia, a large collection of more than 1,000 islands in the South Pacific.

find Park, but instead reported encountering a ferocious band of zombies.[2]

Most people in the 1800s readily viewed primitive peoples as dangerous savages. In the early 1900s, most scientists considered these people inferior to those with a European background. They were seen as children. When Margaret Mead returned from Samoa, she did more than bring back information about the island's teenagers and the way they lived. She helped Americans learn about themselves.

Punk Girl

THE GIRL HER FATHER WOULD CALL "THE original punk," Margaret Mead was born on December 16, 1901. Her father, Edward, called her "punk" until her brother's birth two years later. Then "I was called 'the original punk,' and Dick was known as 'the boy punk,' a reversal of the usual pattern, according to which the girl is only a female version of the true human being, the boy."[1]

Most events in Margaret Mead's life were "a reversal of the usual pattern." She was born when women were not allowed to vote and few attended college. Fewer still had careers.

Margaret's mother was different. Emily Mead studied sociology, attending Wellesley College, a prestigious private university, before graduating from the University of Chicago. It was there that she met Margaret's father, who by then had already written several textbooks on economics and was making a name for himself. Margaret recalled that he told her how he saw her mother "sitting in the front row of a class at the University of Chicago and sat down beside her, announcing (probably only to himself, but we never knew for sure), 'I am going to marry you.'"[2]

Married with children, Emily Mead continued working tirelessly to earn women the right to vote and equality in society. She even refused to give her daughter a middle name. That way, when Margaret got married she could keep Mead as her middle name after taking the last name of her husband.

Unconventional Youth

During the early 1900s, few people owned cars. Many homes lacked electricity or indoor plumbing. Yet in a few decades car ownership, and even air travel, would be common.

Margaret was a child of the new century. She

had the privilege to be born in a hospital—in fact she was the first child born at Philadelphia's West Park Hospital. As she grew older, she wished she was more like other children who had been born at home.

Margaret compared herself to them all the time because she was so different. By the time she reached high school, she had spent less than three years inside a classroom. Other than a year of kindergarten and eighth grade, along with half days in fourth, her education took place outside of a conventional school.

Margaret at approximately one year old, 1902.

Margaret's father worked as an economics professor at the University of Pennsylvania's Wharton School of Business. Her mother continued postgraduate work through a fellowship at Bryn Mawr College. Even as a very small child, Margaret would tell visitors to their home, "My father majored in economics and minored in sociology and my mother majored in sociology and minored in economics."[3]

This seemed like the best way to explain the couple's differences as well as their compatibility.

Margaret grew up believing anything was possible, that she could be anything she wanted to be. The only limits were her own imagination and her abilities.

Margaret was raised by two bright women who seemed to accomplish whatever they set their mind to. Like her mother, her paternal grandmother was educated and accomplished. Despite her unconventional background, Emily Mead had a fairly conventional life. Hers was a traditional marriage in which she was responsible for the household upkeep and her husband expected to be the center of attention whenever he came home. "When my father entered the house, my mother's and my grandmother's absorption with the children was likely to be interrupted by his immediate demands," Margaret recalled in her autobiography.[4]

The familiar nursery rhyme describes little girls as "full of sugar and spice and everything nice." In the early 1900s, most girls fit that description perfectly. They wore starched petticoats beneath full skirts. Even as children they were expected to behave like "proper young ladies." That meant not acting like boys— playing rough or being athletic. Emily Mead thought that was ridiculous. She dressed her daughter in practical clothes so she could climb trees and explore. Margaret was treated differently than most other children and remembered that, at four years old, "I was treated as a full person whose opinions were solicited and treated seriously."[5]

Despite the advantages of her upbringing, Margaret often felt at a disadvantage. Besides wishing she'd been born in a house like her friends, she also wanted to go to school with them. Even the friends she made she did not get to keep for very for long.

Her family rarely stayed put.

She once added up the moves. She claimed

that by the time she entered eighth grade, her family had lived in sixty houses and employed over one hundred different cooks.[6]

Although Edward Mead taught his students how to succeed as businessmen, he was spectacularly unsuccessful. In his lifetime, he embarked on dozens of enterprises. None of them made money. What they did make were demands: demands on his time and energy. They were partly why the Meads were always moving. He needed to live near the mines, farms, and other struggling businesses he owned.

Every fall and every spring, the family lived in the same house in Hammonton, New Jersey, surrounded by five acres of blueberry bushes. In the winter they lived in Philadelphian rental houses near the university. In the summer and during parts of the rest of the year, they lived all over the Northeast while her father tended his struggling businesses and opened small satellite schools for his university.

Because she did not attend school, Margaret

worked even harder to make friends quickly. In each new place, she watched the children her age, noticing the way they spoke and the way they dressed. Then she tried to fit in. Her quiet observations as the "new kid" were crucial steps toward what would become her life's work.

Family life could be chaotic. Her parent's marriage was a struggle: "Certainly there were occasionally very different women in his life. One of them had red hair, and one almost persuaded him to marry her," Margaret remembered.[7]

Instead, Edward tried to make up for his infidelities with expensive presents. Emily always wanted to donate the money to her favorite charity.

Maybe because of these conflicts, Margaret's first stop whenever she came home was the quiet sanctuary of her grandmother's room. No matter where they lived, it was the best room in the house. It got the most sunlight and often sported a fireplace. Surrounded by antiques and mementos collected during a lifetime, Margaret would listen while her grandmother told her stories about growing up during the Civil War. She told of a younger sister who had risked her life keeping the flag safe from Confederate troops when they raided their town.

Martha Ramsey Mead described her college years, when she met Margaret's grandfather. She graduated in the morning and gave the graduation address. That afternoon, Giles was introduced as her husband before he gave his own graduation address. Together the couple traveled across the Midwest, Giles working as a superintendent, his wife Martha as a teacher. Edward was their only child; when he was six his father died. Two days later, Martha took Giles's job as principal, which was highly unusual for a woman in the late 1800s.

As a boy, Edward had moved often. He repeated this pattern with his own family. Later, Margaret would see it as a good example of how the way we live as children can determine our lives as adults.

Margaret Mead is photographed here with her father, Edward, and brother, Richard, in 1910.

Religion

Although her grandmother was a devout Methodist, Margaret's parents were agnostic. Agnostics consider the existence of God a possibility, but lack a personal belief in his existence. Margaret had one brother, Richard, and two sisters, Elizabeth and Priscilla (Katherine, a third sister, died in infancy). The children were left to discover for themselves which religion, if any, worked best for them. It was a thoroughly modern and very unusual practice for the early 1900s.

Other children might have skipped going to church altogether. Instead, Margaret embarked on a thorough tour of a number of them, attending services and Sunday school with her friends. Margaret decided to become an Episcopalian. "Almost at once I felt that the rituals of the Episcopal Church were the form of religious expression for which I had been seeking," Margaret recalled in her auto-biography. "I had not been looking for something to believe in, for it seemed to me that a relationship with God should not be based on what you believed but rather on what you felt."[8]

Four days before her eleventh birthday, Margaret was baptized. Although her father made fun of her, he took the family to the service in his horse drawn carriage. Her parents never quite figured out "how to deal with a child who insisted on fasting during Lent, but then agnostics never know what to do with post-agnostics."[9]

Margaret's parents sometimes disagreed with her choices, but they still encouraged her to make them.

Alternative Education

Although she did not influence Margaret's choice of religion, her grandmother was still influential in the girl's unconventional

Margaret and Richard Mead on the beach in Nantucket, Massachusetts, in the summer of 1911.

education. Wherever they lived, Margaret had tutors. After she became interested in painting, a professional artist gave her lessons. When she needed to study chemistry or biology, a scientist often helped her. Her grandmother covered the fundamentals. She taught Margaret to value books and to write well.

Martha Mead believed children should be exposed to complex math before learning how to add and subtract. Margaret was studying advanced algebra when most children her age were starting grade school. Going to school in the fourth grade, she began the year behind the others, but in less than a few months was at the top of her class. It would become a familiar place for Margaret.

Even before she was a teenager, Margaret thought seriously about what she would do for a career. Like many kids, she had a number of ideas. Although she considered everything from being a veterinarian to being a school teacher, she mainly believed she would be a writer. She spent many quiet hours parked beneath a shady tree writing short stories or working on a novel.

As a teenager, she even helped her mother in her work towards a doctorate. Intelligence testing was very popular with academics in the early 1900s. The Intelligence Quotient or IQ test had its roots in a request by the French government of Alfred Binet to uncover children who were unable to benefit from mainstream learning. Revised by Lewis Terman at Stanford University when Margaret was fourteen, the Stanford-Binet is still the standard intelligence test in the United States.[10]

When Margaret's mother was doing her research, eugenics—a now discredited theory—was also popular. The theory suggested that certain races were less intelligent than others. Emily Mead and her daughter traveled into the immigrant communities around the family's New Jersey home in an effort to discover whether or not language training affected the IQs of the children of Italian immigrants.

Margaret finally enrolled in full-time classes

when she reached junior high. The tiny Buckingham Friend's School was run by the Quakers and boasted less than three dozen students between the ages of ten and twenty. For the most part, the older children helped out the younger. Academically she shined in the small, personal environment.

"All our books were at least two generations old," she remembered. "We studied Latin from the same grammar [book] that my grandmother had studied. . . most of what I learned, I learned from the old-fashioned schoolbooks themselves or from Grandma, who continued to help us with our lessons."[11]

High school was much more difficult.

After the family moved to Doylestown, where her father ran a farm, she began attending the local high school. The transition was

Margaret Mead drew this self-portrait when she was thirteen years old.

25

difficult. Margaret loved learning. She enjoyed discovering new things and conducting experiments, but most of her classmates did not.

"Going to school offered no challenge. No one had to study very hard," she recalled, "and if there was good ice and a bright moon, we all went ice skating."[12]

Most of the students were raised in families typical for the time. Margaret's parents were far more liberal. In the small farming town, they stood out.

Her unorthodox learning had left gaps in her education. As in fourth grade, Margaret started out behind her classmates in most subjects but was soon at the top of her class.

Another year, 1918, and another move—to New Hope, Pennsylvania. There, she enrolled at the private Holmquist School, part of an artist's colony. It was a place Margaret remembered fondly as having "as many teachers as students and we had a precious diet of exciting teaching and religious exploration under one of the founders who also taught religion at Bryn Mawr."[13]

Margaret graduated from there the next year. She only wanted two things: to go to college and to get married. Neither would work out exactly the way she had planned.

Rushing

ACROSS EUROPE THE GREAT WAR (LATER known as World War One) was raging. Sparked by the assassination of the Archduke Franz Ferdinand, the conflict had drawn in the armies of Austria-Hungary and Germany in battles with France, England, and the United States. On June 17, 1917, civilians nervously watched the shoreline. There were rumors that a German U-Boat had been spotted off the coast of New Jersey.

For Margaret Mead the date had a different significance. She would always remember it as the first time she fell in love.

George Cressman, a science teacher at Doylestown High School, was giving the commencement. He invited his younger brother

Luther to tag along. Twenty years old and tall, with a brilliant shock of red hair and bright blue eyes, Luther made a strong impression on fifteen-year-old Margaret.

Before the night was over they had danced together, and she told him he was "just about right." Although they did not see each other regularly, they wrote to each other often and their relationship grew.

The attraction only intensified after Luther announced he would enroll in divinity school after graduating from Pennsylvania State College. He would become an Episcopal priest. "It was what his mother had always wanted him to do, and a minister's wife was what I wanted to be," Margaret later explained.[1]

Religion was now an important part of Margaret's life. It was easy for her to imagine marrying someone with his own congregation. She envisioned herself as a successful writer, married to Luther and raising half-a-dozen children.

Her parent's liberal ideas extended to

marriage. They didn't want their daughter married until she graduated from college.

Off to School

Her mother had attended Wellesley. Margaret might have had different ideas about religion and marriage, but she thought she would follow the same path academically. Then her father made a confession. He was broke. Bad business decisions had finally caught up to him. He couldn't afford the high tuition of any of the private colleges Margaret had in mind. Besides, it would be a waste of money since all she was going to do was get married.

"Look at those useless little hands," her father wailed. "Never did a day's work in their life and never will. You'd maybe make a good mistress, but a poor wife. You'd better study nursing!"[2]

Margaret was heartbroken. She also thought it was a poor excuse—her own mother had gone to college, married, and had a large family.

Emily Mead's conventional choices did not keep her from intellectual pursuits.

How could Edward Mead encourage his wife's ambitions while discouraging his daughter's? Ironically, her mother had left Wellesley after her own father's financial problems. Now it looked like Margaret wouldn't even get there in the first place.

Margaret Mead and her first husband, Luther Cressman, in 1918.

They compromised. Margaret would go to
college, but instead of an Eastern university, she
enrolled at Indiana's DePauw University, where
her father had completed his undergraduate
education.

She imagined college as being filled with
intellectual debate, both in the classrooms and
the dorms. Her dreams of late-night discussions
about philosophy, literature, and politics
evaporated once she reached DePauw. Young
women who came across as intelligent and
confident were treated as poorly there as they
had been at Margaret's first high school.

Mead's accent marked her as an Easterner.
Her confident answers proved she was an
outsider. Most of her classmates had grown up
on farms where they were often the first member
of their family to go to college. The women
seemed to be trying to earn a "Mrs. degree;"
they wanted to meet their future husbands and
go from being a "Miss," to a "Mrs." Instead of
intellectual conversations, her peers spent their
free time rooting for the school's football team

or trying to become a member of a sorority or fraternity.

Sorority Life

Sororities are female-only clubs (fraternities are the male-only version), that admit members based in part on the prospective member's looks, family background, personality, and special abilities such as athletics or academics.

Like today, in the 1920s some schools were

An early twentieth century photograph of the campus of DePauw University in Indiana.

considered "Greek" dominated schools, where fraternities and sororities make up a sizeable percentage of the school's population. These schools are often large, state-run colleges with successful football programs. Since many campus social activities are organized by the groups, life can be pretty lonely for students who don't become members.

Margaret decided to "pledge," or join a sorority. It would be an adventure. "During the summer, I began to receive letters from an effusive girl who lived in the town where Aunt Beth [Upton lived]. The girl explained that she was a Kappa [Kappa Gamma] from DePauw and that she was looking forward to inviting me to a Kappa party when I arrived at college."[3]

During "rush week," prospective members— "rushees"—attend various parties at the large houses where the fraternities and sororities are located. They hope to get a "bid," an offer to pledge their loyalty to a sorority.

Although Margaret went with high hopes, the Kappa party was a disaster. She arrived in an "unusual and unfashionable dress that was designed to look like a wheat field with poppies blooming in it." The young woman who had invited her took one look at the outfit and did not say another word to Margaret all evening.

"I found the whole evening strangely confusing," Margaret later admitted. "I could not know, of course, that everyone had been given the signal that inviting me had been a mistake. Afterward, my two roommates got the bids they expected, but I did not get a bid."[4]

Mead may not have realized that sororities were not just popular at DePauw. They were practically invented there.

The first sorority (or Greek-letter fraternity for women) began in the United States at DePauw in 1870. Betty Locke, a student at DePauw (then called Indiana Asbury University), tried to pledge her brother's fraternity. The gentlemen told her she could not rush, but she could be their mascot. She declined the invitation.

Frustrated, she went to her father. He

suggested she start her own organization. From a group that included Locke and just three of her friends, sororities in the United States were born. Like fraternities, they have secret rituals, and in addition to social activities, they also perform charity work. Today there are thousands of sorority chapters across the United States, similar in many ways to the first organization.

Author Alexandra Robbins explains in her book *Pledged*, "Kappa Alpha Theta served as a support network to the female students who were treated poorly by male students, faculty and friends at a school that had only begun to admit women three years before."[5]

By the time Margaret Mead was admitted to DePauw, sororities were a crucial part of the campus life. Not belonging to one did not just exclude her from many social activities, girls in sororities would not even say hello to her. She had never felt so isolated and confused in her life.

Her father never realized what a hard time

his daughter was having until he warned her that he could not afford to bring her home for Christmas. Tearfully, she admitted she wanted to quit. She knew what a failure that would be, but couldn't he at least let her come home for the holidays?

Edward Mead found the money.

When she returned very little had changed. All her life, Margaret Mead had adapted to her environment. Suddenly she found herself unable to adapt. As winter's chill faded into spring, she made a decision. She was leaving DePauw.

The Rise of the Ash Can Cats

THROUGHOUT MOST OF THE 1900S, IVY League schools like Columbia, Harvard, and Princeton did not admit women. From the early 1800s, female-only schools like Bryn Mawr, Mount Holyoke, and Wellesley (Emily Mead's alma matter) offered an equally demanding education. The Seven Sisters, as they were called after organizing in 1927, included Barnard College, which was on the Columbia University campus in New York, New York.[1]

Margaret Mead managed to get her father to keep his promise. He had told her if DePauw did not work out, she could go to school back East. Things had not worked out, and although Wellesley was still too expensive, her father agreed to Barnard. It was not only less expensive, it was also close to where Luther Cressman was in divinity training.

She had found her place. Without worrying about men's opinions, the young women answered confidently in the classroom. Engaged to Luther Cressman, she would not have to worry about finding a boyfriend.

In a way, Mead created her own sorority. Although its admissions were less formal and exclusive (just living in the same apartment was invitation enough), the group had its own secret rituals and even a motto. "Never break a date with a girl for a man," were the words they tried to live by.[2]

For a time the residents of Apartment 21, 606 West 116th Street, traveled under a variety of names. Then a clever and well-loved professor named Minor Lathom gave them the name that stuck. "You girls who sit up all night readin' poetry come to class lookin' like 'Ash Can Cats,'" he declared. From that time on, the group lived with the nickname used to describe dirty alley cats.[3]

The Roaring 20s

The Ash Can Cats shared apartments in and around Harlem throughout the three years of Mead's undergraduate time at Barnard. The then predominantly African-American neighborhood

A graduation ceremony is held on the grounds of Barnard College in 1909. Margaret Mead attended Barnard as an undergraduate student from 1920 to 1923.

was home to numerous nightclubs, including the world famous Apollo and The Cotton Club.

It was an era writer F. Scott Fitzgerald called "The Jazz Age." After World War I, Americans were ready to celebrate. Although the 19th amendment gave women the right to vote, the 18th amendment had taken away the right to drink. Alcohol was made illegal—it was prohibited. Despite the law, it was still abundant.

All-night bars, called "speakeasies," served cold liquor and hot jazz as young people danced the Charleston and women wore slinky, loose dresses. The trendsetting woman of the time was described as "a daring, even naughty tomboy. The 'flapper' of the 1920s was high-spirited, flirtatious and often reckless in her search for fun and thrills."[4]

In the 1920s, as today, older people complained about the younger generation's taste in music, their provocative dancing, and their scandalous clothes.

"We belonged to a generation of young women who felt extraordinarily free—free from the demand to marry unless we chose to do so, free to postpone marriage while we did other things, free from the need to bargain and hedge that had burdened and restricted women of earlier generations," Mead later explained in her autobiography. "We laughed at the idea that a woman could be an old maid at the age of twenty-five, and we rejoiced at the new medical care that made it possible for a woman to have a child at forty.

We did not bargain with men."[5]

For many, Greenwich Village was the cultural center of the country, the heart of the Jazz Age. (Fitzgerald, among other noted writers, lived part of the time in New York.) And while she enjoyed the nightlife New York offered, she also embarked on more literary adventures. One May, she and the other Ash Can Cats hung a basket of flowers from the door of their favorite poet, Edna St. Vincent Millay.

Margaret later claimed to have seen forty plays in just her first semester at college, embracing all New York had to offer even while pursing a traditional marriage. Cities are "a place where there is no need to wait for next week to get the answer to a question," Mead said in her last book. "It is that place where one need never be bored, where there is always the possibility of a new encounter that may change one's life."[6]

Besides their late night adventures, the group encouraged each other's artistic pursuits and comforted each other during relationship struggles and academic challenges. While her friendships in The Ash Can Cats may not have helped her decide what she wanted to do with her life, it did help her figure out what she did not want.

It was during this time that she let go of an ambition she had held for nearly half her life.

She planned to be a writer. But when one of her fellow "cats," Leonie Adams, began getting her poetry published while still in college, Mead realized her own literary gifts paled in comparison. She wanted a career, not a hobby. She did not want Luther to support her while she struggled to get published.

It was time to find another dream.

Discovering Anthropology

"I wanted to make a contribution [to society]," she later explained in her autobiography. "It seemed to me then—as it still does—that science is an activity in which there is room for many degrees, as well as kinds, of giftedness. It is an activity in which any individual, by finding his own level, can make a true contribution. So, I chose science—and to me that meant one of the social sciences. My problem then, was which of the social sciences."[7]

By her senior year, Mead was preparing for a career as a psychologist. The profession was hugely popular, in part due to pioneering psychoanalysts Sigmund Freud and Karl Jung. Their theories on everything from human sexual drives to dreams and the subconscious were widely debated both in the pages of popular magazines and during late-night discussions amongst Mead's friends.

Mead was planning to pursue a masters degree in psychology when a lucky accident altered her life. She had to choose between a pair of very popular senior level courses. One was in philosophy, the other in anthropology. Had she chosen the philosophy course, the world might never have heard of Margaret Mead.

The Smithsonian Institute's Anthropology Department defines anthropology as "the science that deals with the origins, physical characteristics and cultural development of humankind."[8] It is the study of human variation—how people developed their different behaviors, cultures, and societies. She would later praise it for cutting through the "stupid underbrush of the nineteenth-century arguments based on ethnocentric superiority," the idea that people from a white European background are superior.[9]

It is a profession of observing. She was first exposed to a form of anthropological research by her mother, who kept nearly a dozen notebooks charting Margaret's development.

It was not, necessarily, the most obvious path

for a young woman who needed to be the center of attention. By her senior year, many had noticed the way the energy in a room changed whenever she entered. Men seemed to fall in love with her purely from the sharpness of her intellect. More obviously pretty women were ignored in favor of Margaret. Then again, she always wore her glasses whenever she went out dancing. She did not listen to people who told her she would look better without them—she needed them for people watching.

She was, one friend later recalled, "a missile waiting to be directed—she was going to be something; it didn't so much matter what."[10]

She found her place in Columbia's cramped and overcrowded anthropology department. At the time, it consisted of only two small offices and a seminar room in the journalism building. The course was taught by Franz Boas, a passionate instructor whom Margaret would describe half a century later: "On one side [of his face] there was a long dueling scar from his student days in Germany—an unusual pursuit for a Jewish student—on which his eyelid drooped from a recent stroke. But seen from the other side, his face showed him to be as handsome as he had been as a young man. His lectures were polished and clear."[11]

Anthropology was at a crucial crossroads.

Trapped by Expansion

There are many ways to learn about other societies. Ancient cultures often leave artifacts behind. In the Americas, Mayans, Incas and Aztecs built monuments and temples before their cultures were destroyed.

For groups still in existence, observation was one of the best ways to learn about them. As Margaret Mead prepared to graduate from Barnard, anthropologists were frantically making contact with these groups. They were running out of time.

In certain remote parts of the world, groups lived untouched by modern society. Everything from their clothing to their traditions to their language had been largely unchanged for centuries. Just as certain species were driven to extinction after modern society breached their territory, primitive cultures were equally threatened by twentieth century expansion.

Modern exploration techniques were opening up areas once too dangerous or remote for study. This meant anthropologists could observe societies that had had little contact with the outside world.

Sadly, this ability also threatened a way of life. Cultures that came into contact with the outside world were forever changed. They started wearing baseball caps and Western clothes. They developed a taste for soda pop. Worse, they slowly lost their connection to the past as language and traditions evaporated.

Time was running out, Boas explained in his lectures. The anthropologists of the early twentieth century had one last chance to record the details of ancient cultures before they disappeared forever.

Although Margaret admired Boas, she really connected with his assistant. Ruth Benedict was

Ruth Benedict would prove to be one the strongest influences on Mead during her college years.

a bright and thoughtful woman fifteen years older than Mead. Benedict was so shy her lectures to the class were often hard to follow. Yet, she shared Boas's passion for the subject and, one-on-one, did better at convincing others to pursue it as a career.

After her divorce, Benedict mainly dated women, but in the beginning, her relationship with Margaret was more like an older aunt than a girlfriend.

Despite the differences in the two women's personalities, they formed a deep friendship. Boas could be intimidating, and Benedict answered Mead's questions as best she could.

In a profession with few women, it was Ruth Benedict who inspired Margaret Mead's career choice. During lunch one afternoon, Benedict quietly explained that "Professor Boas and I have nothing to offer but an opportunity to do work that matters."[12]

Work that matters. That settled it for her. What else was there?

5

Radical Dreams and Traditional Choices

EDWARD MEAD FINALLY MADE A GOOD investment. The ten thousand dollars he spent on Margaret's education produced a young woman who graduated from Barnard College in 1923 with a degree in Psychology and who was invited to join Phi Beta Kappa, a prestigious honor society. In the 1920s, ten thousand dollars was twice what the average person earned in a year, but he offered his daughter another ten thousand dollars for an around-the-world trip. All she had to do was postpone her wedding.

Margaret Mead refused. She was stubborn and committed. Following her June graduation, the wedding was less than three months away and no one who knew her—not her closest friends nor her family—understood why she was going through with it. While earning his divinity degree, Luther was less than one hundred blocks away, but for all the time the couple spent together, he could have been back in Pennsylvania.

To Mead, her fiancé was stable and kind. Although already considering a more adventuresome life, she decided she still wanted to be a minister's wife. Of course, some quietly wondered if she was more interested in a lavish wedding ceremony than a lifetime commitment.

As much as her stubbornness about the marriage distressed her father, Margaret's choice to keep her own last name shocked him deeply. Her mother's decision to not give her daughter a middle name would be unnecessary. "I'm going to be famous some day," she argued, "and I'm going to be known by my own name."[1]

Luther accepted her decision far more quietly. But then his calm nature—in contrast to her father—was a big reason she was marrying him.

On the morning of September 2, 1923,

Margaret Mead made a frantic call to her fiancé. She had just seen his family at the hotel. The young woman who a few years before had been rejected by a sorority for her own fashion sense asked, "Luther, your family's not coming to the wedding in those clothes are they?"[2]

Luther made sure they changed before the ceremony at the Episcopal Church in Lahaska, Pennsylvania. He did not even get upset, but then Luther did not get upset easily. He took it in stride when she slept in a separate bedroom on their honeymoon so she could work on a book review. And he was not even bothered by her habit of giving the keys to their first apartment to friends from college who needed a place to meet their boyfriends.

The only thing that really angered Cressman was reading in her autobiography fifty years later that she considered him to be her "student husband."

"We were both students," he explained, "she just as much as I. We weren't trying some innovative social experiment, the way she may have wanted it to seem in retrospect; we were getting married the way any other couple would. But all her life Margaret had a way of saying, 'Well, if that isn't the way it was, that's the way it should have been.'"[3]

Revisiting the Past to Move Forward

Twenty-one when they wed, Margaret took a focused approach to her career and a more casual one to her marriage. Even as she worked towards her masters in psychology, she was contemplating her doctorate in anthropology. And even as she and Luther set up housekeeping, most of their private moments were interrupted by friends who dropped by or spent weeks living off of their sofa.

Margaret realized that the more she studied anthropology, the more it related to psychology. The work she did in psychology connected to the work she had done with her mother nearly ten years before.

For her crucial masters thesis, she revisited Emily Mead's research on immigrant families and intelligence testing. Margaret administered an intelligence test to 276 Italian children. "There were many tiresome statistics to do," she remembered, "as I correlated the scores on intelligence tests with the amount of English spoken in their homes [by their parents]."[4]

Her efforts in psychology would soon inform her work as an anthropologist. Referring to her work she advised "extreme caution in any attempt to draw conclusions concerning the relative intelligence of different racial or nationality groups on the basis of tests."[5]

Similar conflicts were occurring in the field of anthropology. Even as she delivered her masters thesis, *Intelligence Tests of Italian and American Children*, she was contemplating how certain groups of people are viewed.

Deep divisions had developed between anthropologists and psychologists such as Sigmund Freud, whose book *Totems and Taboo* compared members of primitive cultures to children.

Mead's anthropology professor Franz Boas found the idea deeply insulting, especially as it

Mead studies a book in a library. The more Mead studied anthropology, the more she saw how it related to psychology.

came from someone who had never done field work and had formed his opinions from books he read and a formal education that concluded the century before. Rather than look at primitive cultures as childlike, Boas suggested a more important issue was "the way in which personality reacts to a culture. . . . Courtesy, modesty, good manners, conformity to definite ethical standards are universal, but what constitutes courtesy, modesty, good manners and ethical standards is not universal. It is instructive to know that standards differ in the most unexpected ways. It is still more important to know how the individual reacts to these standards."[6]

While some, like Freud, believed we all follow predictable patterns, others, like behaviorist J. B. Watson, disagreed. He suggested that how children are raised and their environment and conditions as they grow up determine how they behave as adults.

Margaret Mead already could see that in her own family, the way her grandmother's travel influenced her son's frequent moves and her granddaughter's wanderlust. The question was whether or not such behaviors are truly environmental—perhaps such traits were handed down from generation to generation like blue eyes. Maybe even if Margaret had been the adopted child of a stable family she would have grown up to dream of world travel.

Finding Her People

Boas helped focus her ideas. For her doctorate, instead of comparing different groups of people across the world, Margaret would examine the differences among closely related groups. She chose Polynesia, the large triangle of islands stretching across the South Pacific from Hawaii to New Zealand in the Southwest and to Easter Island in the Southeast. Surrounded by ocean, the island's natives developed in isolation until European explorers reached them in the 1700s.

Comparing the closely linked histories of different islands, she chose to examine what many consider a stable element of their culture: tattoos. She studied the tattoos of Hawaiians, Maori, Tahitian, Marguesan, and Samoan cultures. During the 1924 convention of the British Association for the Advancement of Science in Toronto, Canada, Mead presented her preliminary work. She also began thinking about finding her own "people."

The young anthropologists who clustered around Boas's office often talked about their "people"—the culture they had adopted for intensive study. This was the group that formed the backbone for their research papers and books; Mead wanted her own. For a while it looked like her people would be the American Indian.

Although American Indians were still popular with researchers, by then most of them lived in modern conditions and usually were connected to the outside world. Mead worried that she would not have much to contribute.

The way tribal life had been altered by the outside world had already been well documented. Worse, the groups had become so accustomed to being studied that they often charged money for interviews, and a running joke of the time was that every family had a mother, father, two children, and an anthropologist.

At the conference she formed a close relationship with Edward Sapir, a forty-year-old anthropologist. She was enchanted by his stories about the adventures he'd had exploring foreign lands. She returned to New York City feeling like a race car revving its engine at the starting line.

The work she was doing for her doctorate was no more adventuresome than the statistics she compiled for her masters. The only place she was traveling was the university library. Mead wanted adventure and risk. She wanted to leave the country and find her own people in a remote location. She wanted to actually go to Polynesia. Unfortunately, such an exploration could be very dangerous. Tropical diseases were rampant and often fatal, and some tribes were occasionally violent. Although for the most part such practices as cannibalism had faded due to the influence of missionaries, they were not unheard of.

Mead also had to overcome concerns based on her gender. She was a married woman, and no one wanted to deal with an angry widowed husband. Plus, women sometimes got pregnant, not a good physical condition when you are in the jungle with weeks or months away from contact with the outside world.

Boas was old-fashioned, and his approval was necessary for Mead to go anywhere. He wanted her to study a tribe in the Western United States. Since he was the one overseeing her doctorate and providing the grant money she would need to travel, his refusal seemed to end all discussion.

Other people might have given up. Mead was not like other people.

Finding Approval

She was determined not to let anything—or anyone— get in her way. When Boas again resisted, she turned to her secret weapon:

Dr. Franz Boas (above) originally resisted Mead's request to study in Polynesia. He had preferred that she study American Indian tribes in the United States.

Edward Mead. When it was an argument between her and her father, he always resisted her choices. Now, however, an outsider was telling her what to do. It did not matter that Margaret Mead was a twenty-three-year-old married woman pursuing an advanced degree. As far as Edward Mead was concerned, no one else could tell his daughter what to do. That was his job. If Boas refused to give Mead's daughter funding for the trip, then he would give her the money himself.

Just as it looked like Margaret Mead was going to go one way or another, Boas was ready with a compromise. Working at Clark University, Boas found himself in a heated conflict with his boss. The head of anthropology, G. Stanley Hall, believed biology was responsible for the conflicts of adolescence.

Teenage rebellion is not new, not to the new millennium generation, nor to their parents. It did not begin in the 1960s with hippies rebelling against their parents, nor with Frank Sinatra inspiring screaming young girls called "bobby soxers" in the 1940s. And although the Ash Can Cats might have disagreed, it did not begin in the 1920s either.

Boas wondered if the difficulties of our adolescence are actually "unavoidable periods of adjustment through which everyone has to pass."[7] This was the prevailing view of the time among psychoanalysts like Freud. It was a "eureka moment" for Boas when he realized that sending a woman to study adolescent girls in a primitive environment would help decide if adolescent rebellion is universal. He was sure that he would get better information from young women than from young men, whom he suspected would not be as revealing.

Suddenly Margaret Mead's gender was an advantage. Although she was excited by the opportunity, he warned her she should expect to "waste a great deal of time just sitting about and listening but I should not waste time [studying the larger culture]."[8] And instead of the island she chose, which was very remote, he told her she should go to Samoa, which had a U.S. Naval base and was less dangerous. Mead agreed.

The best way to find out if there were common experiences connecting everyone as they grew up was to examine a variety of cultures. Mead was finally on the way to doing just that.

6

Coming of Age

"SAMOA WAS NOT CHOSEN BECAUSE I HAD any theoretical or personal preference for it over other Polynesian islands," Margaret Mead later wrote. She had never been that interested in the challenges of growing up either, until Franz Boas asked her to help answer the questions, "Are the disturbances which vex our adolescents due to the nature of adolescence itself or to civilization? Under different circumstances does adolescence present a different picture?"[1]

In an interview with Mead nearly fifty years later, anthropologist T. George Harris pointed out, "There were all these theories around. . . that claimed to apply to all mankind. You went after the single negative, one culture where the theory broke down."

Interviewer J. Diener agreed, saying, "Sure, one negative is worth a thousand positives. It kills the theory."[2]

Mead just needed that one negative. In the United States, regardless of race or background, the teenage years were almost universally a time of rebellion. The period that Mead called "storm and stress" was marked by conflicts with those in authority: parents, teachers, and other adults. Many believed the root cause was biological; coping with hormones and their changing bodies made it normal that teens would "act out."

But what if there was a culture where the society enabled teens to grow up without all the tension—without the storm and stress? Such a culture could disprove the absolute power of biology. "[If] one society could bring its children through adolescence painlessly, then there was a chance that other societies could do so also," Mead noted.[3]

Mead traveled to Samoa hoping to find out if such a culture existed. Situated twenty-three hundred miles southwest of Hawaii, the eastern portion became a United States territory after World War One (New Zealand managed the western half.) Boas had told Mead to come home if the climate made her ill—the humidity rarely drops below eighty percent, and the temperature hovers between seventy and ninety degrees Fahrenheit, giving rise to all types of deadly bacteria. The rains could be quite oppressive as well.

It was the type of environment anthropologists encounter regularly. Unfortunately, Mead was not a seasoned world traveler. Mead had never spent a day by herself before. Life had always been filled with friends, family, and her husband. Now it would take six weeks for a letter to reach any of them.

Her friends were back home and her husband was in Cambridge, England, working on a theological fellowship. A letter Mead wrote him while she was stopped over in Hawaii reached him soon after he arrived. It promised him she would never leave him unless she "fell in love with someone else." It was not exactly

Reo Fortune took this photograph of Mead in a canoe with Manus children in 1928.

comforting, and decades later he looked back on the period as the worst of his life. He was "a deeply troubled person, one who seemed to have been defeated by life. My marriage seemed to have a very uncertain future." He would soon abandon the priesthood.[4]

A Rough Start

Mead arrived in Samoa with luggage she had carefully organized. Few things are more important than packing the right kind and amount of gear for an anthropological expedition. Since she could not count on help transporting it, she needed to travel light.

She made sure she had netting and repellant, for mosquitoes are carriers of malaria, an often fatal disease. Others had told her the hot, humid environment destroyed silk, so she packed cotton, nothing but cotton—half-a-dozen dresses, stockings, and underwear. She loaded up on notebooks and pens along with a lock box for her money, a small camera, and a portable typewriter—a total of less than two dozen items.

Today an anthropologist's gear can sometimes take up a good bit of the cargo hold in an airplane or boat, as they pack cameras, recording equipment, computers, and various other technical equipment. Yet even today, anthropologists try to pack light, as Laura Tamakoshi notes, "Some people take polaroid cameras for records of events that can be discussed further with informants. It is now popular to use computers in the field but power is a problem in some areas. I prefer the old fashioned notebook which can be shoved in a shoulder bag along with an instant 35 mm camera for easy use."[5]

Expecting adventure from her first day in a foreign land, Mead was sorely disappointed. The officers had little time for the petite woman with big dreams, and their wives looked down on her cheap cotton dresses and sturdy shoes. It turns out they did wear silk in the tropics. She booked a room in a rundown hotel.[6]

Mead might not have had a steady home growing up, but now she was desperately homesick. Like many who have visited foreign lands before and since, she reacted with predictable hostility: she hated the food and the heat, and would later view a sudden destructive hurricane as a personal inconvenience. Although she tried not to get too bored and focused on learning the language, Margaret Mead was restless. She was ready for her life to begin.

Off to Ta'u

After six weeks, she was ready to relocate. There had been some disagreement between her and Boas as to where she would spend the bulk of her time. She wrote convincingly that it should be Ta'u. One of the three islands in the Manu'a group, it was visited every three weeks by a steamship delivering mail and supplies. She pointed out that it "was the only island with villages where there are enough adolescents, which are at the same time primitive enough and where I can live with Americans. I can eat native food, but I can't live on it for six months; it is too starchy." Even better, compared to the rest of Samoa, the island was "unspoiled."[7]

The only nonnatives were the pharmacist and his wife, Edward and Ruth Holt. As an added bonus, the island's chief spoke English.

Boas agreed. It would be the perfect place for her to test his theories. Mead set up her office (and her sleeping quarters) in the Holt's medical dispensary. Although she would be criticized for not living with a native family, she pointed out that sharing a room with over half a dozen others not only eliminated privacy, it would make it harder to get her work done. She needed to ask girls she did not know frank questions about their sexual experiences. The room offered privacy and a ready-made excuse for the twenty-five girls she interviewed. When asked why they were spending time with Mead, they could say they were getting medicine.

Being in the field alone is always "on the job training." Mead later wrote that, in anthropological research, "To do it well, one has to sweep one's mind clear of every supposition." Margaret Mead tried to do exactly that. Every day young women would come to see her. Mead had only "all the courage of complete ignorance."[8]

Using the excuse of intelligence tests, Mead was able to get the girls alone (otherwise they arrived in groups of three). Mead had the advantage of her psychological background. She was good at getting her subjects to be comfortable and open up. No subject was too personal. However, even for a woman of twenty-three, the stories told by girls almost half her age were breathtaking to someone who had grown up in a far more sexually conservative society. The things Mead recorded would be debated for decades.

Sexual Revelations

Although the women were expected to be virgins at marriage, Mead learned that they often tricked their husbands. Instead, many of the women were sexually experienced from a young age. She heard stories of men sneaking into women's beds at night and about the physical relationships they formed with other girls. To Mead, a community that seemed peaceful, where girls were allowed to experiment without being ostracized, seemed like paradise compared to the more rigid moralities of the United States.

Mead heard stories that were quite similar and believed their consistency lent them a credibility. So many young women could not be working so well together to make up such stories.

For over nine months in Samoa, she filled up notebook after notebook. Besides accounts of late-night romantic and other sexual habits, she detailed an unusual practice among the young women she interviewed. When there was tension in their own homes, for whatever reason, the girls would pack up and move in with the families of friends or with extended relatives. There was no disgrace in this, and Mead thought it was an innovative way to avoid damaging conflicts.

As she left the island, Mead had to have seen Samoan practices in her own terms. She would have liked a way to move out of the house during conflicts, or even as a way to stay in one place. The "Samoan compromise" seemed like an ideal way for young people to navigate the rocky shores of adolescence. By living with multiple families, they could find peace. By exploring their own desires at a young age, they could be better prepared to be adults with a single partner. It seemed so much better than the never-ending petty arguments suffered by most teens in the United States. The Samoan method seemed more flexible and promoted self sufficiency while reducing such problems as juvenile delinquency.

Despite her earlier problems with the food and weather, in the end she fell in love with Samoa and its people. Boarding a ship bound for England, the adventure was still fresh, her memories almost romantic. She was not expecting an actual romance. But as the boat took on more passengers in New Zealand, a tall man with a movie star name—Reo Fortune—got on board. In a ship crowded with tourists, he was one of the few who shared Mead's interests. And they had six weeks to get to know each other.

In and Out of Love

DESPITE THE HARD WORK AND THE struggles in Samoa, Margaret Mead's time there was almost a vacation from reality. Traveling to France, where Luther Cressman would be meeting her, she wondered if she could stay married. The two were different in so many ways. Now that he planned to teach sociology, she realized just how different. He would be stable, set in one place, something she thought she wanted. Now she saw herself traveling, going to remote regions. And she did not want to be alone.

She realized how lonely she had been when Reo Fortune boarded the ship. The twenty-three-year-old was doing postgraduate work at Wellington, New Zealand's Victoria University College. Bound for Cambridge University, he was interested in the psychology of dreams. He shared her interests in human behavior. Their relationship became close very quickly. She started recording her dreams for him and they spent long evenings walking along the deck.

Mead had spent nine months away from her husband. Fortune was still nursing the pain from a broken engagement. She would not allow their relationship to become physical. Still, before the six-week voyage's conclusion, they were regularly seated by themselves during meals. Other passengers assumed they were a couple.

On a warm June day in 1926, Luther Cressman waited anxiously at the dock in Marseilles, France. Watching carefully as the passengers disembarked, he worried he would miss his petite wife in the crowd. Even after the passengers had come ashore, he continued to wait—wondering what had happened to Mead.[1]

His wife was still inside, so focused on her conversation with Fortune that she never noticed the ship docking. When she realized what had happened, Mead quickly gathered her things and rushed to her husband. Fortune followed, trying to act casual. "That is one of the moments I would take back and live differently, if I could," she later admitted in her autobiography. "There are not many such moments, but that is one of them."[2]

Shattered Dreams and New Beginnings

Cressman and Mead's reunion was not pleasant. At the hotel that afternoon, she admitted to falling in love with someone else. The prediction in the letter was coming true.

By the time Mead and Cressman reached New York City, the marriage was more or less over. Divorce was far less common in the 1920s than it is today. Mead was not as concerned with society's expectations, but she listened to her friends. Although they had never considered Luther a good choice for her as a husband, they thought it was unfair for her to leave him for another man. So, the couple continued to live together while Luther taught sociology and Mead began writing a book about her experiences in Samoa.

With Cressman's change in career plans, Mead's dreams of being a minister's wife vanished. Her hopes for a large family evaporated even faster after a doctor's visit. That fall she learned she had a tipped uterus. Her physician warned her she would never carry a

Margaret Mead on crutches in the Pere Village, 1928.

child to term; any pregnancy she had would end in a miscarriage. "One of my principal reasons for not wanting to marry Reo was my feeling that he would not make the kind of father I wanted for my children," she later admitted. "But if there were to be no children. . . ."[3]

In June of 1928, she went to Mexico, where getting a divorce was less complicated than in the United States.

Despite the challenges of her personal life, her professional life became more than she could have hoped for. After being rejected by Harper Brothers, a fellow anthropologist, George Dorsey, suggested she take her book to a friend of his. William Morrow's company was small and unknown, but it would soon become one of the most powerful publishing companies in the U.S. When he read Mead's manuscript, titled *Coming of Age in Samoa*, he saw its potential. However, in order to attract the largest possible audience, he suggested she tailor it to American readers by connecting the Samoan experience to the experiences of teenagers in the U.S.

Mead quickly agreed. After all, the storm and stress of American adolescence was part of what prompted her to make the journey to Samoa in the first place. Adding three chapters to the book, she reached the conclusion that "if a society could be found in which the growing boys and girls missed out on all the storm and stress, then the anthropologist would know. . . that storm and stress was not inevitable."[4]

In other words, biology was not destiny—the culture was the determining factor. Applying what she learned in primitive cultures to life in the U.S. would become the pattern of her work.

In New York City, Mead finally found a permanent home. It was not in an apartment building or a house. It was in a museum. In 1926, she was appointed assistant curator of ethnology at the American Museum of Natural History. Her office was inside the tower, an area that had once served as living quarters for scientists. Although she would be promoted and offered a nicer office below in the main section, she worked from the tower for most of the rest of her life. The office was away from the hustle and bustle of the museum, and it gave her plenty of room for the items she brought back from her trips.

Back to the Islands

During her time at Barnard, Mead and her fellow Ash Can Cats spent many late nights discussing the controversial theories of Sigmund Freud. In Samoa, she began comparing the theories he formed in Vienna with real-life situations. Her work there had been with teenagers. However, since Freud had compared primitive people to children, it made sense to study the children of primitive people.

She set off to explore the Manus, a "preschool tribe," as she called them, on the north coast of New Guinea. It was not as joyful as the trip to Samoa had been. She arrived a newlywed; Fortune insisted they marry before the trip. The two found the people of Manus quite unpleasant. A formerly warlike tribe, they were policed by the Australians, who had pretty much ended their savagery. However, without the fighting, they put their energy into complex trades, requiring gifts from each other for all types of things. They demanded cigarettes for interviews.

"They were a puritanical, materialistic, driving people and they were driven relentlessly by their ghostly mentors," she later wrote. "The ghosts punished people for not meeting their innumerable economic obligations, and if they had not met them, for not contracting new ones. Life for the Manus was very much like continually walking up a down escalator."[5]

The biggest surprise to Mead was how good-natured the children were. "[They] were delightful, but I always had before my eyes the kind of adults they would soon become."[6] She saw this as helping disprove a developing theory of education—that given the freedom to flourish, all children would become caring, creative adults.

During much of her stay, Mead was sick with malaria. She quickly found out how

Margaret Mead carries Piwen, a Manus girl, on her back in 1928.

unsympathetic her new husband was. He expected others to suffer in silence, like he did. He was never as kind as he had been on the cruise ship, and Mead actually felt grateful she could not have children.

For all the difficulties, it was while in New Guinea that Mead received some startling news. She had done something very few anthropologists ever do. She had written a best-selling book.

Coming of Age in Samoa was not written in the complex academic style of most anthropology books. Instead, Mead wrote it not just for other anthropologists but for young people, parents, and anyone who could benefit from her examination of teenage behavior. By relating the lives of Samoan teens to those in the United States, she touched on a popular topic. She also discussed sex in frank and fairly explicit language when few other books did so.

Because of her choices, not only did the book sell well, but Mead also became one of the best-known anthropologists in the world. Yet the unexpected money and fame also made her even more of a target for those who disagreed with her conclusions.

Critical Backlash

They attacked her for viewing the society as "gentle, uncompetitive and guilt free," when Samoans were really "driven by rivalry and rank, and that they suffered from 'musu,' which Mead described as an expression of 'unwillingness and intractability,' whereas [other anthropologists]. . . found it to be a form of destructive rage, often leading to suicide, particularly in adolescence, a period which Mead described as 'the age of maximum ease' in Samoa."[7]

Pointing to examples like her misuse of the word 'musu,' they wondered if her interpretations were based more on faulty translations of Samoan than any real breakthroughs in research.

Perhaps the most personally painful criticism came from fellow anthropologists who said her youthful naiveté allowed her to be duped by the Samoan girls. This view was highlighted by anthropologist Derek Freeman, who seven decades later interviewed a number of the young girls Mead had spoken with.

Freeman believed that the young women, embarrassed by the personal nature of the interviews, engaged in a practice called 'ula,' or recreational lying. As one of Mead's subjects, Fa'apua'a explained, "As you know, Samoan girls are terrific liars when it comes to joking, but Margaret accepted our trumped-up stories as though they were true."[8]

Even in Mead's time, they wondered how she could claim that teenage girls were so sexually active when, by her own figures, just over half had had any activity. This figure was not radically different from girls of the same age in the United States. Further, if a dozen or so of the girls had been sexually active without any form of birth control, there should have been at least a pregnancy or two. There were none.

Perhaps for Mead, worse than criticism of her research, her second book was criticized for her writing. Her first book might have been a breakthrough, but many reviewers saw *Growing*

Up in New Guinea as the labored efforts of a writer trying to find her style while not repeating herself. It was not entirely successful. Some critics felt she reached too much for her conclusions; others were bored by the repetitive nature of the book and the way she seemed to be working too hard to find connections between the Manus and Americans.[9]

Maybe Mead just had a harder time writing effectively about a place and a people she disliked.

If the Manus of New Guinea were unpleasant, her next expedition was even worse.

After earning her doctorate from Columbia, her dissertation on "An Inquiry into the Question of Cultural Stability in Polynesia" was published in Germany. She decided to follow it up with research of a Native American tribe, the Omaha of Nebraska. In the summer of 1930, Ruth Benedict convinced Mead and Fortune to spend a few months studying the Native American tribe. After studying remote cultures that had been relatively untouched by outside influences or other anthropologists, the tribe was a blend of cultures. Trying to write up her study, she complained in a letter to Ruth Benedict, saying, "I had no sense of values left when I try to evaluate this work."[10]

Shortly after her work on the Manus was published, Mead met another man. Not long after returning to New Guinea with Fortune, she

Anthropologist Gregory Bateson, whom Margaret Mead met shortly after publishing her work on the Manus.

began hearing stories about anthropologist Gregory Bateson. English born and Cambridge educated, he came from a long line of researchers and academics. His father, William Bateson, was very influential in the early study of genetics.

"You're tired." It was reportedly Bateson's first words to Mead when he met her. The two simple words had a profound impact; they suggested awareness and sympathy. Her husband was darkly handsome, but also incredibly aloof. No matter how sick she got, he seemed unable to give her an ounce of compassion. Now this lanky, six-foot-five anthropologist was paying attention to her. He was, in the words of another anthropologist, "the most physically unattractive man I've ever known," but he was kind and a good listener. He had even read Mead's book on the Manus and asked her detailed questions about it.[11]

Just as her marriage with Cressman had been in trouble when she met Fortune, her marriage with Fortune was troubled when she began spending time with Bateson. In 1934 she met him in Ireland; the next year she made plans to work with him in Bali. By then she was divorced from Fortune.

Even as she filed for her second divorce, Mead saw another window of opportunity swiftly closing. The impact of the modern world had been a growing threat to primitive societies. In the middle 1930s, the modern world was moving towards war and the threat reached every region Mead wanted to study.

8

The World at War

MARGARET MEAD'S DESCRIPTIONS OF places like New Guinea and Samoa did more than open up an unknown world to thousands of readers. Her arguments against viewing primitive tribes as "children" also helped change a popular belief. For decades, European colonists had described such people as the "white man's burden." Mead's writing led many to see how all humans are connected and how the challenges we face are similar. Her work voiced an early opposition to eugenics, the theory that some races are genetically superior to others.

Mead's dreams were finally coming true. She was beginning to find success and fame in her profession. An ocean away, a man named

Adolph Hitler was pursuing his own darker dreams.

Hitler wanted to restore German pride after his country's terrible defeat in World War I. As part of the Versailles Treaty, in the 1920s countries that began World War I like Austria-Hungary and Germany were expected to pay for the damage they caused. The costs were enormous. Because so much money went to repay war costs, prices rose in Germany. Eventually, one week's wages could barely buy a loaf of bread.

Hitler, a failed painter, appealed to people who wanted a strong government and someone to blame for the country's problems. He focused on the Jews, many of whom were in successful middle-class professions like law and banking. Although they were not in control of the country's economy by any means, enough people believed they were to give Hitler credibility. He also directed his venom toward other minorities like gypsies, the mentally ill, and homosexuals.

Eliminating those who Hitler considered inferior would lead to the world domination by the Aryan "ideal": blonde-haired, blue-eyed men and women who could prove they did not have a trace of Jewish blood.

In 1923 he led a failed rebellion against the government. While serving nine months in prison, he began writing down his theories about the Aryan race and German pride in the book *Mien Kampf* or My Struggle.

After his release, he began to attract more ardent supporters. In 1932 his National Socialist Party—the Nazis—won the majority of seats in the Reichstag, the German Parliament similar to the U.S. Congress. The next year Hitler was appointed prime minister. Given emergency powers to end unrest, he eliminated free speech and free press and began jailing those who opposed him.

In 1938 he defied a treaty and reunited Germany with Austria. The next year his army marched into Poland. England declared war, but soon the German army would also occupy

Adolph Hitler's eugenic rants were directly opposed to the research and views put forth in the writings of Margaret Mead.

Poland, Holland, and France—an American and British ally. Germany would also align with Italy and with Japan, which was slowly invading countries along the Pacific Ocean.

Unlucky in Love

As Hitler's Nazis marched across Europe, in the United States Mead realized her own explorations were coming to an end. From 1936 to 1939 her new husband, Gregory Bateson, had accompanied her to New Guinea, where she had previously worked with Fortune. Like Fortune, Bateson shared Mead's profession if not her fame. Mead and Bateson had greatly contrasting styles—a difference that would eventually be a problem.

"It was almost a principle of pure energy," Bateson later recalled. "I couldn't keep up and she couldn't stop. She was like a tugboat. She could sit down and write three thousand words by eleven o' clock in the morning and spend the rest of the day working at the museum."[1] She felt settled and comfortable with him in a way she had not with Fortune. She even believed he would make a good father, a bitter-sweet realization for someone unable to have children.

Then a miracle happened.

She had been pregnant before. Although birth control was available by then, mistakes happened, and in primitive lands it was not always available. Just as the doctors predicted, her pregnancies ended early.

Until 1939.

Miraculous Conception

"One of the complications in the field is the difficulty of knowing whether you are, or are not, pregnant," she later explained about the return from Bali. In Chicago she arranged a test. "The result was negative. I was heartbroken."

However, back in New York, she still felt peculiar. She took the test again and found out she was pregnant. No one had told her drinking alcohol could interfere with a test, and she had had drinks the night before her test in Chicago.[2]

From that moment on, she took every precaution to ensure a successful pregnancy.

She even consulted a young pediatrician named Ben Spock who shared many of her views about childbirth. He would go on to worldwide fame as Dr. Spock, writing a series of books for parents.

Mead had only described parenting, but on December 8, 1939, she finally became a parent with the birth of her daughter, Mary Catherine Bateson. It was amazing timing. Any trips abroad would be nearly impossible—U.S. forces would soon establish bases on New Guinea, and Europe had became a battlefield.

Mead might not have made a living as a poet or a novelist, but she was a writer nevertheless. The year her daughter was born, Mead's other children—her books *Coming of Age in Samoa, Growing Up in Samoa* and *Sex and Temperament* were packaged in a single volume, *From the South Seas*.

Working with Frances Cook Macgregor, she also published a book that used her husband's photographs and described their work in Bali— *Growth and Culture: A Photographic Study of Balinese Culture.*

In Demand

The year of her daughter's birth, she began working as a visiting lecturer at Vassar, a respected women's college. Although her theories and writing style were debated by other anthropologists, colleges across the country began inviting her to speak and awarded her honorary degrees. The first of many came from Wilson College in Chambersburg, Pennsylvania, in 1940. She was also given an achievement award from the Chi Omega sorority, a bittersweet honor given her own struggles with sororities.

From the time *Coming of Age* was first published, she was in great demand as a speaker. Audiences of anthropologists and lay people were equally eager to hear her stories of life on the South Pacific island. Often her harshest critic sat in the front row.

"He wore a cutaway frock coat, a vest trimmed with heavy white braid, a stand-up collar with a stick pin in his cravat, and pink coral studs in his hard boiled shirt front. He wasn't a particularly jovial fellow, and often glared at her over rimless spectacles," recalled former student Patricia Grinager. Later he would tell Mead, "You're too short. Speak up but don't do it from behind a podium. . . . You talk too fast. Don't move your head back and forth and spout over the tops of folks like a lawn sprinkler."[3]

This audience member was her father, Edward Sherwood Mead, at once her biggest fan and harshest critic. As wartime and child rearing curtailed her travels, her lecture schedule increased.

Wartime

On December 7, 1941, Japanese forces attacked the United States naval base in Pearl Harbor, Hawaii. The United States declared war against Japan and her allies Germany and Italy.

In the United States, the effort to support the war required strict rationing of a number of products, from rubber to gasoline. New cars were not made in favor of jeeps and tanks. In the midst of so much death, Mead was focused on life. Just as her mother had, she kept notes of her daughter's development.

Despite being a wife and mother, Mead's life was never conventional. She worked steadily and relied on a variety of acquaintances to help with

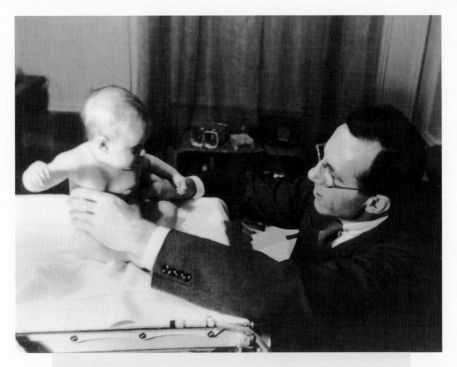

Margaret Mead's daughter, Mary Catherine Bateson, is examined by another fellow authority in his chosen field, Dr. Benjamin Spock, in 1940. Spock was considered an expert on child-rearing at the dawn of the baby boom generation.

child care. And like most people in the U.S then, she did all she could to help in the war effort. She served as executive secretary of the Committee of Food Habits of the National Research Council. She also used her writing skills, authoring pamphlets for the Office of War Information.

Mead began to look at the United States as she had looked at primitive societies. After so many years of travel, staying in her home country made her reflective. In 1942, the same year her mentor Franz Boas died, her book *And Keep Your Powder Dry: An Anthropologist Looks at America* was published. Written in three weeks, the book was inspired in part by the motto found on the change in our pocket: *E pluribus unum,* out of one, many. The most important goal the U.S. should have is building, "from a hundred cultures, one culture which does what no culture has ever done before—gives a place to every human gift."[4]

In the book she compared the United States with the seven other cultures she had studied. The book expressed her hope that her country could use its brains and values to help the rest of the world. In the end, she felt helping other countries this way would also help our own— perhaps even ending wars.

A few years later, the United States had its chance. Having defeated Germany, Japan, and Italy, the United States was alone among the allies in not having suffered extensive damage. The continental United States was never attacked, whereas England would spend years repairing the damage from numerous bombs. With more resources available, the United States spent millions of dollars and many years rebuilding countries like Japan and Germany, former enemies that became stable democracies thanks to U.S. help.

At home, Mead tried to repair her relationship with the first man she had felt compatible with. Bateson had spent much of the war in England, but the separation had not helped their relationship. Unfortunately, in 1950 Mead's third marriage ended in divorce. She was a single mother in an era when that was rare. But new worlds awaited.

New Worlds and Old

WAR CHANGES EVERYTHING. IT ERASES borders and ends lives. It alters civilizations and changes the course of history—for history is written by the winners. In the twentieth century no conflict affected more lives across the planet than World War II. Even primitive societies located thousands of miles from the combatants were changed.

In 1953 Margaret Mead decided to document the impact of World War II on a culture she had studied. "I feel closer to a people who believe they can remake their culture if only they have the will to do so," she wrote a friend.[1] The Manus in New Guinea had done exactly that after their island was used as a U.S. air base during conflicts in the Pacific.

Although Mead was divorced, she was never alone. For her return trip to New Guinea, Mead brought along Ted and Lenora Schwartz, an anthropology student and his nineteen-year-old wife. Now in her early fifties, Mead had gained weight and benefited from the energy and enthusiasm of her young partners. She also left behind her thirteen-year-old daughter.

Mead would be gone for nearly a year, something that Mary Catherine Bateson tried to accept. Her mother, after all, belonged to the world.

On the island, Mead learned surprising things about both the Manus and their interactions with the Americans. Almost every native she interviewed had good things to say about the soldiers they encountered. They were respectful and giving, much more so than their Australian counterparts had been.

Sometimes, far from home and in unfamiliar surroundings, soldiers have been known to take advantage of local women. Mead reported that

Margaret Mead, Lenora Schwartz, and Theodore Schwartz (left to right) are seated behind a group of Manus children in 1953.

not one child was born with an American father and a Manus mother.

Although the soldiers did not leave any children behind, they left many other things. They gave the Manus wristwatches and baseball caps, radios and ball-point pens. The outside world had arrived quite violently, and they quickly incorporated the Western goods into their own culture, just as they incorporated Christian beliefs into their own after the missionaries arrival.

The Manus had become "potential members of the modern world, with ideas of boundaries in time and space, responsibility to God, enthusiasms for the law."[2]

Mead's book *New Lives for Old* described the changes she witnessed and expressed hope for the other native cultures that would inevitably be touched by modern society. By the time she returned to the United States, her star was rising.

Ahead of Her Time

Beginning in the early 1950s, she had been giving a series of lectures at New York City's New

School for Social Research, and she continued speaking after her return. Her opinions were, as always, ahead of their time.

As she had during the war, Mead turned her critical eye on Americans. She felt especially qualified to discuss the challenges of marriage—and divorce. "We have to face the fact that marriage is a terminable institution," she had once told a reporter.[3] The longer people live, the less likely they are to stay with one person for the rest of their lives. Her quote predated the explosion in divorce rates by a good decade.

"Any woman can find a husband unless she is deaf, dumb or blind," she had told her audience during her New School lecture in 1950, but "she cannot always marry the ideal man of her choice."[4]

An Ideal Partner

Perhaps Mead's ideal husband would have been a combination of the three she had married— with Luther's stability, Reo's passion, and

Bateson's skills as a father. Then again, in later life, Mead's ideal partner was not a man at all. In the mid-1950s Mead began living with Rhoda Bubendey Metraux, a younger woman, in New York's then-bohemian Greenwich Village. The two co-authored the book *Themes in French Culture*.

The relationship was far less turbulent than the ones she had with men. It also lasted longer; in the 1960s they were still living and writing together, co-authoring a series of articles for *Redbook* magazine.

Since many people at that time would have condemned the relationship, Mead kept it secret. However, she had no problem speaking her mind on other issues, from race to war to women's rights. As she grew older, the thickness of her body and her gray hair made her seem like a grandmother, which was beneficial when she approached controversial subjects. The 1960s were nothing but controversial subjects.

She lectured against the Vietnam War and for Civil Rights. In 1971 she and celebrated

Rhoda Metraux (left) with Margaret Mead (right).

African-American author James Baldwin co-authored *A Rap On Race*. In 1969 she finally retired from the museum. She used her extra time to pen her memoirs, *Blackberry Winter*, which was published in 1972. In 1977, Mead was diagnosed with pancreatic cancer; she died on November 15, 1978. The next year she was awarded the Presidential Medal of Freedom.

Fifteen years earlier, she told the *New York Times*, "I was brought up to believe that the only thing worth doing was to add to the sum of accurate information in the world."[5]

Like another Jazz Age author, F. Scott Fitzgerald, Mead's fame was larger than the work she did. While Fitzgerald's fiction explored the landscapes of early twentieth-century America, Mead's nonfiction described regions few people had heard of, let alone visited. When Fitzgerald died, much of his work was out of print, his fame a memory. Since being published in 1928, *Coming of Age in Samoa* has never been out of print, and Mead's early fame never

Mead co-authored *A Rap On Race* with celebrated African-American author James Baldwin (above) in 1971.

diminished. Now considered a classic, it was reissued in 2001 with a new forward by Mary Pipher, the bestselling author of *Reviving Ophelia*.

She viewed anthropology as not some dry science devoted to studies of other cultures, but as a living, breathing tool for promoting human understanding—by examining other cultures, we can better understand ourselves.

Activities

Margaret Mead traveled thousands of miles to learn about people whose lives were radically different than our own. Today, most young people have the opportunity to interact with people whose childhood and adolescence were just as different. These people are probably no more than a phone call away.

Interview a grandparent, another older relative, or a neighbor about a variety of issues. The report can be narrowly focused—such as clothing styles of the 1940s or musical tastes of the 1950s—or more broad ranging—examining how children were treated in the middle twentieth century. As you begin to weave together your report, you can supplement what you learn from interviews by utilizing magazines and newspapers from the era to learn about everything from dating habits to religion.

Chronology

1901—Margaret Mead is born on December 16 in Philadelphia, Pennsylvania, to Emily and Edward Mead.

1912—The *Titanic* sinks after hitting an iceberg.

1914—World War I begins; ends with the Treaty of Versailles four years later.

1919—Mead enrolls at DePauw University in Indiana.

1919—F. Scott Fitzgerald becomes a best-selling author at twenty-three when *This Side of Paradise* is published.

1920—Mead transfers to Barnard College.

1922—Mead enrolls in an anthropology course taught by Franz Boas.

1923—In March, Mead discusses pursuing a doctorate in anthropology.

1923—Mead graduates from Barnard with honors in June; is admitted into Phi Beta Kappa honor society.

1923—Marries Luther Cressman in Buckingham, Pennsylvania.

1924—In August, she presents her paper on "Rank in Polynesia." Meets Edward Sapir who motivates her to study primitive tribes.

1925—Passes her doctoral examinations at Columbia (will finish her doctoral thesis years later, in 1929).

1925—On August 31, Mead arrives on the island of Pago Pago in American Samoa.

1925—Reaches Ta'u, where she will do most of her field work, on November 9.

1925—Is appointed assistant curator of ethnology at the American Museum of Natural History.

1926—On January 1, a destructive hurricane ravishes Ta'u.

1926—Boards *S.S. Chitral* in Sydney, Australia, where she will meet Reo Fortune.

1928—Mead signs a contract with William Morrow and Company for the book *Coming of Age in Samoa*.

1928—Signs divorce papers from Luther Cressman on July 25.

1928—Marries Reo Fortune in Auckland, New Zealand, on October 8; does fieldwork with him on Manus.

1929—Returning to New York in September, Mead discovers she is now a celebrity.

1939—Adolph Hitler's Nazi Army invades Poland.

1939—Daughter Mary Catherine Bateson is born.

1941—On December 7, Japanese forces attack the U.S. Naval base on Pearl Harbor, Hawaii.

1942—Franz Boas dies in New York City on December 21.

1945—World War II ends.

1950—Divorces Bateson.

1969—Neil Armstrong becomes the first man to walk on the moon.

1972—Autobiography *Blackberry Winter* is published.

1974—Mead becomes president of the American Association for the Advancement of Science.

1978—Margaret Mead dies of pancreatic cancer on November 15.

Chapter Notes

Chapter 1. The First Storm

1. Margaret Mead, *Letters from the Field 1925–1965* (New York: Harper and Row, 1977), p. 43.

2. "The Mystery of Mungo Park," 2001, <http://www.fvza.org/mungo.html> (October 17, 2005).

Chapter 2. Punk Girl

1. Margaret Mead, *Blackberry Winter: My Earlier Years* (New York: Kodansha International, 1995), p. 20.

2. Ibid, p. 23.

3. Margaret Mead, *A History of Psychology in Autobiography* (Englewood Cliffs, N.J.: Prentice-Hall, 1974), p. 295.

4. Ibid., p. 30.

5. Jane Howard, *Margaret Mead: A Life* (New York: Simon and Schuster, 1984), p. 22.

6. Ibid., p. 21.

7. Mead, *Blackberry Winter*, p. 35.

8. Ibid., pp. 76–77.

9. Mead, *A History of Psychology in Autobiography*, p. 300.

10. *dyslexia@bay*, n.d., <http://www.dyslexia-at-bay.com/textpage.htm> (October 17, 2005).

11. Mead, *Blackberry Winter*, p. 78.

12. Ibid., p. 80.

13. Ibid., p. 85.

Chapter 3. Rushing

1. Margaret Mead, *Blackberry Winter: My Earlier Years* (New York: Kodansha International, 1995), p. 84.

2. Ibid., p. 85.

3. Ibid., p. 87.

4. Ibid., pp. 94–95.

5. Alexandra Robbins, *Pledged* (New York: Hyperion, 2004), p. 281.

Chapter 4. The Rise of the Ash Can Cats

1. "What Colleges Make Up the 'Seven Sisters'?" *Ask Yahoo!*, January 8, 2002, <http://ask.yahoo.com/ask/20020108.html> (October 17, 2005).

2. Margaret Mead, *Blackberry Winter: My Earlier Years* (New York: Kodansha International, 1995), p. 108.

3. Jane Howard, *Margaret Mead: A Life* (New York: Simon and Schuster, 1984), p. 43.

4. Allison Lurie, *The Language of Clothes* (New York: Random House, 1980), p. 74.

5. Mead, *Blackberry Winter*, p. 108.

6. Margaret Mead, *World Enough: Rethinking the Future* (Boston: Little Brown, 1975), p. 42.

7. Mead, *Blackberry Winter*, p. 111.

8. "Introduction," *Anthropology on the Internet for K–12*, n.d., <http://www.sil.si.edu/SILPublications/Anthropology-k12/auth-k12.htm> (October 17, 2005).

9. Margaret Mead, *Continuities in Cultural Evolution* (New Haven, Conn: Yale University Press, 1964), p. x.

10. Howard, p. 52.

11. Mead, *Blackberry Winter*, p. 113.

12. Ibid., p. 114.

Chapter 5. **Radical Dreams and Traditional Choices**

1. Jane Howard, *Margaret Mead: A Life* (New York: Simon and Schuster, 1984), p. 60.

2. Ibid., p. 61.

3. Ibid., p. 62.

4. Margaret Mead, *Blackberry Winter: My Earlier Years* (New York: Kodansha International, 1995), p. 122.

5. Margaret Mead, *American Journal of Sociology*, 31:5, March 1926, p. 667.

6. Margaret Mead, *Coming of Age in Samoa* (New York: Perennial Classics, 2001), p. xxii.

7. Ibid.

8. Mead, *Blackberry Winter*, p. 138.

Chapter 6. **Coming of Age**

1. Margaret Mead, "Social Organization of Manu'a," *Bernice P. Bishop Museum Bulletin 76* (Honolulu, Hawaii, 1930; reissued 1969), p. 476.

2. J. Diener, "A Conversation with Margaret Mead and T. George Harris on the Anthropological Age," *Psychology Today*, April 1970, p. 66.

3. Derek Freeman, *Margaret Mead and Samoa: The Making and Unmaking of an Anthropological Myth* (Cambridge, Mass.: Harvard University Press, 1983), p. 73.

4. Jane Howard, *Margaret Mead: A Life* (New York: Simon and Schuster, 1984), p. 75.

5. "Anthropology Fieldstudy Developed by Professor Tamakoshi of Truman State University," *Truman State University*, n.d., <http://www.truman.edu/academics/ss/faculty/tamakoshil/> (October 17, 2005).

6. Phyllis Grosskurth, *Margaret Mead: A Life of Controversy* (New York: Penguin Books, 1988), p. 27.

7. Margaret Mead, *Letters from the Field 1925–1965* (New York: Harper and Row, 1977), p. 28.

8. Grosskurth, p. 25.

Chapter 7. **In and Out of Love**

1. Jane Howard, *Margaret Mead: A Life* (New York: Simon and Schuster, 1984), pp. 90–96.

2. Margaret Mead, *Blackberry Winter: My Earlier Years* (New York: Kodansha International, 1995), p. 162.

3. Ibid., p. 164.

4. Derek Freeman, *Margaret Mead and Samoa: The Making and Unmaking of an Anthropological Myth* (Cambridge, Mass.: Harvard University Press, 1983), p. 76.

5. Ibid., p. 171.

6. Ibid.

7. Phyllis Grosskurth, *Margaret Mead: A Life of Controversy* (New York: Penguin Books, 1988), p. 34.

8. Derek Freeman, *The Fateful Hoaxing of Margaret Mead* (Cambridge, Mass.: Harvard University Press, 1983), pp. 139–140.

9. Grosskurth, p. 41.

10. Howard, p. 154.

11. Mead, *Blackberry Winter*, p. 208.

Chapter 8. **The World at War**

1. Jane Howard, *Margaret Mead: A Life* (New York: Simon and Schuster, 1984), p. 253.

2. Margaret Mead, *Blackberry Winter: My Earlier Years* (New York: Kodansha International, 1995), p. 248.

3. Patricia Grinanager, *Uncommon Lives: My*

Lifelong Friendship with Margaret Mead (New York: Rowman and Little, 1999), p. 51.

4. Margaret Mead, *And Keep Your Powder Dry* (New York: William Morrow, 1975), p. 256.

Chapter 9. New Worlds and Old

1. Phyllis Grosskurth, *Margaret Mead: A Life of Controversy* (New York: Penguin Books, 1988), p. 69.

2. Margaret Mead, *New Lives for Old: Cultural Transformation—Manus 1928–1953* (New York: William Morrow, 1975), p. 56.

3. Harvey Breit, *The New York Times*, VII, October 30, 1949, p. 41.

4. Margaret Mead, "Modern Women's Dilemma," lecture at the New School for Social Research, 1950.

5. "Mead, Margaret, Quote about Learning," *Yahoo!*, August 9, 1964, <http://education.yahoo.com/reference/quotations/quote/48665> (June 13, 2006).

Glossary

adolescence—Time of psychological and physical development between childhood and adulthood.

anthropologist—Scientist who studies the origins of physical, social, and cultural behavior in humans.

conservative—Favoring traditional views and values.

culture—The form of civilization at a particular time, including its beliefs, arts, and government.

eugenics—Science that studies how to improve a species genetically. Once used for suggesting racial superiority among some groups.

philosophy—The study of the source of human knowledge.

psychology—Science of mind, emotions, and behavior.

primitive tribes—Groups whose culture has existed intact for centuries without outside influence.

sorority—Female-only social and charitable organization.

speak-easy—Illegal bar or nightclub during Prohibition.

Further Reading

Horn, Geoffrey M. *Margaret Mead*. Milwaukee: World Almanac Library, 2004.

Howard, Jane. *Margaret Mead: A Life*. New York: Fawcett, 1990.

McDonough, Yona Zeldis. *Sisters in Strength: American Women Who Made a Difference*. New York: Henry Holt, 2000.

Pollard, Michael. *Margaret Mead: A Biography.* Westport, Conn. Greenwood Press, 2003.

Ziesk, Edra. *Margaret Mead*. Broomall, Pa.: Chelsea House, 1990.

Internet Addresses

**Margaret Mead: Human Nature and
the Power of Culture**
http://www.loc.gov/exhibits/mead/

**American Museum of Natural History:
Margaret Mead**
http://www.amnh.org/exhibitions/expeditions/
treasure_fossil/Treasures/Margaret_Mead/
mead.html

Anthropology on the Internet for K-12
http://www.sil.si.edu/SILPublications/
Anthropology-k12/index.htm

Index